WALES

LANDMARKS, LANDSCAPES & HIDDEN TREASURES

Publisher and Creative Director: Nick Wells
Senior Project Editor: Catherine Taylor
Art Director: Mike Spender
Layout Design: Jane Ashley
Digital Production: Chris Herbert
Copy Editor: Anna Groves
Proofreader: Amanda Crook

Special thanks to Taylor Steinberg

FLAME TREE PUBLISHING
Crabtree Hall, Crabtree Lane
Fulham, London SW6 6TY
United Kingdom

www.flametreepublishing.com

First published in 2015

15 17 19 18 16
1 3 5 7 9 10 8 6 4 2

© 2015 Flame Tree Publishing

ISBN 978-1-78361-420-2

A CIP record for this book is available from the British Library.

Every effort has been made to contact image copyright holders. We apologize in advance for any omissions
and would be pleased to insert the appropriate acknowledgement in subsequent editions of this publication.

Printed in Singapore

WALES

LANDMARKS, LANDSCAPES & HIDDEN TREASURES

Michael Kerrigan

FLAME TREE
PUBLISHING

Contents

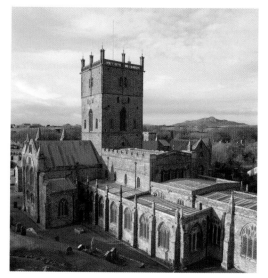

View from the Sugarloaf,

South Wales **184**

Introduction

**'There is no corner of Europe that I know ... which so moves
me with the awe and majesty of great things as does this mass of
the Welsh mountains seen from this corner of their silent sea.'**

Thus wrote Hilaire Belloc, looking landwards from his yacht off Anglesey to the rugged coastline and the yet more rugged heights behind. To the Anglo-French writer they may have seemed 'great things', but Welsh historian Jan Morris reminds us that Snowdon, the highest of these peaks, at 1,085 metres (3,560 feet), would hardly qualify as a foothill in any serious mountain range. Morris' own characterization of her homeland is double-edged: Wales is 'damp, demanding and obsessively interesting'. A wet blanket at Belloc's party of praise? Perhaps, and yet it's true that what's really intriguing about Wales is not so much the immediate view – however stunning – as the sense of what's behind. What makes Wales' appeal 'obsessive' is the sense of history that haunts every land-, sea- and streetscape, the poetic possibility that resonates in every view.

Belloc knew full well that the Alpine peaks above the Italian city of Udine were well over four times the height of Snowdon; he just felt that this view of North Wales was more dramatic. Scale is all-important here. Jan Morris, who subtitled her famous 1984 book *The*

Matter of Wales 'epic views of a small country' was in no doubt that, when it came to Wales, less was more. 'It is a small country', she acknowledged,

> '… in many ways the archetype of a small country, but its smallness is not petty. On the contrary, it is profound, and if its frontiers were ever to be extended, or its nature somehow eased, its personality would lose stature, not gain it.'

It helps, of course, that these narrow borders contain such a rich and rewarding variety of landscapes. The mountains, lakes and valleys of Northwest Wales are just the start. To the east, towards the English border, the contours of the country are less starkly dramatic, but by no means less beautiful. The Clwydian Hills have the uncompromising character of a much more rugged range; they have an impact out of proportion to their size – like Wales itself. Amidst the hills, in green and leafy vales, little rivers run through picturesque market towns. Again, there's that sense of disproportion: this part of Wales seems so much more picturesque than it has any business being – perhaps it comes of being overlooked so long. Mid Wales brings more mountains, but more mystery as well. How did what should have been the country's most accessible region come to be so wild – the 'Green Desert' of Wales? Conversely, the puzzle in West Wales is how this, perhaps the remotest corner of the Principality from England, should have been its most obviously anglicized. All the wildness of this part of Wales seems to be concentrated in its coastline, in which jagged cliffs, vertiginous stacks and rocky islands alternate with luxurious beaches of golden sand.

South Wales is similarly a land of contrasts, with gentle lowlands like the Vale of Glamorgan on the one hand and upland areas like the Black Mountains on the other. Here, though, there are also contrasts between the natural loveliness of the countryside and the – perhaps more contested – beauties of Wales' three main cities, all of which are to be found on this southern plain.

At times, during the last century, it must have seemed as though industrialism had permanently blighted much of South Wales. Even then, that would have been an exaggeration: Cardiff, Swansea and Newport are all surrounded by pleasant countryside. As for the Valleys, with their crowded colliery communities, they were indeed just that: valleys, with wild and beautiful upland ridges on either side. In any case, one viewer's 'blight' has always been another's treasure: a new generation is rediscovering South Wales' industrial past as heritage. And why not? As elsewhere in the British Isles, the most seemingly 'natural' landscapes have been marked by human occupation or exploitation: the walling off of fields; the grazing of sheep; the felling (or planting) of forests; the flooding of valleys for reservoirs. Time is a great healer and, as centuries go by, that antique colliery with its winding gear may look no more out of place than a fifteenth-century humpback bridge. There is, indeed, an entire book to be written on the mark human technology has made on Wales. Between the standing stones of Pentre Ifan Dolmen, in the Preseli Hills, and the Millennium Bridge in Swansea is the engineering expertise of fifty-five centuries.

Great works like the Menai Bridge and Pontcysyllte Aqueduct are great monuments of civil engineering, but Wales' early history was one irrevocably marked by war. The traditional Anglo-Saxon view of the Welsh as indomitably warlike is as reductive as any stereotype. That said, their country's challenging topography seems to have strengthened the spirit of a people who did indeed fight tooth and nail for their freedom. Even when that freedom was lost, the Welsh were slow to relinquish their independent-mindedness. When the Romans came here in the first century AD, they established a major legionary fort at Caerleon, north of Newport, and built a network of forts and roads crisscrossing the whole country. The extent of this legacy is deceptive, however; a testament less to the successful 'Romanization' of the country than to the difficulty of keeping it controlled.

Though the Vikings came and went at will during the ninth and tenth centuries, they contented themselves with coastal raiding. Even so, they made their mark. Their incessant raids cut short a vigorous monastic tradition which had made busy cultural and commercial centres of what are now backwaters like Bardsey Island in the north and Llantwit Major in the south. In the centuries after 1066, however, the Anglo-Norman barons could only secure the border-country (the 'Marches') and the far southwest. Further north, especially in the ancient northwestern kingdom of Gwynedd, native princes continued to hold sway. Prince Llywelyn ap Gruffudd, with his brother Dafydd, resisting English attempts to force them back into the far northwestern corner of their country, went to war with Henry III of England and his Welsh allies in 1255. An uneasy peace ensued until, taking advantage of instability in England, Llywelyn broke out and extended his rule over almost the whole country. Henry recognized his status as Prince of Wales in 1267.

Five years later, however, Henry was succeeded by his son Edward I, whose patience with a wayward Wales was soon exhausted. In 1277, starting out from Chester, striking first at Flint and then pushing on through what is now Denbighshire to Llywelyn's heartlands in the west, Edward soon suppressed the Welsh; until under Llywelyn's younger brother, Dafydd, they rose up again in 1282. Llywelyn and his vassals joined in, and this time round the war was much more closely fought. Finally, though, Edward's sheer strength and soldierly experience prevailed. Defeating Llywelyn's army at Orewin Bridge near Builth Wells, Mid Wales, he marched north into Snowdonia, taking Llywelyn's headquarters at

Dolwyddelan Castle by storm. In the years that followed, Edward surrounded Northwest Wales with a chain of castles – Conwy, Carnarfon, Harlech.… Impressive monuments then and still intimidating to this day.

The spirit of rebellion, so strong in the Welsh till now, seems to have been quelled by the events of 1282. Whilst Edward's reputation as the 'Hammer of the Scots' didn't prevent that people from keeping up the fight with England for a further three hundred years, the Welsh dragon seems to have slumbered from this time on. Yet to suggest that the Welsh had been fundamentally subdued by this defeat would be to ignore the evidence of the country's extravagant artistic life. Welsh patriotism found expression in language, in bardic poetry, in song and dance. To this day, Welsh nationalism tends to articulate itself more clearly in the cultural sphere than the (more explicitly political) nationalism of Scotland. The institution of the bard – a peripatetic poet, harpist and singer, something like the minstrel or the troubadour of wider European tradition – had passed into obsolescence around the end of the Middle Ages. As an idea, however, he lived on. Indeed, the bardic tradition was to be revived in early-modern times: the first great eisteddfods – grand festivals of bardic poetry and Welsh culture – were held in the eighteenth century.

By this time, South Wales was industrializing apace. In so doing it was diverging culturally from the rest of Wales. The miners of the Valleys – team-workers, bound together by the roughness and the danger of their lives and their heritage of reformed Protestantism, naturally coalesced into male-voice choirs. Big cities, like Cardiff, brought together immigrants from other countries – especially from Ireland and England, who introduced customs and traditions of their own. The post-War era has brought further waves of immigration, and seen important structural and economic developments that have changed the face of Wales. However, none of these has compromised its deeper identity. This is still a tightly knit village of a country, as proud of its friendliness and warmth as it is of its patriotic history and, of course, of its incomparably beautiful valleys, hills and coasts.

Northwest Wales

From the craggy heights of Snowdonia to the storm-lashed coasts of the Llŷn Peninsula, from the secret glades of Betws-y-Coed to the open waters of Lake Bala, the northwestern corner of the country is Wales at its most wild. So it's no coincidence that it is also Wales at its most Celtic.

Seven centuries ago, Gwynedd was the last Welsh kingdom to hold out against the English. It was from here that Prince Llywelyn ap Gruffudd and his brother Dafydd sallied forth against the forces of Edward I. Their defeat saw Wales annexed by the

English Crown. To this day, though, the region has remained a cradle of Wales' ancestral culture. Welsh is widely spoken – for many, indeed, it's the first language. Yet this independence, this patriotism, this waywardness of spirit, made Northwest Wales the focus for a longstanding English presence of which King Edward's castles are only the most visible symbol. The most quintessentially Welsh of regions, Northwest Wales is at the same time full of reminders of just how complex a historical and cultural creation the Welsh identity is.

Menai Suspension Bridge
MENAI BRIDGE, ANGLESEY

Right. Built by Thomas Telford in 1826, the Menai Bridge is not only an extraordinary engineering achievement but also a monument to the pioneering days of the railway age. The crossing between Holyhead and Ireland might have been used for thousands of years but westward traffic out of England had gone by sea from Chester (and, later, Liverpool). What seems to us now a natural corridor along the North Wales coast to Anglesey was no such thing in former centuries, when overland transport was difficult and arduous. This route was really only opened up in modern times.

Plas Newydd
LLANFAIRPWLLGWYNGYLL, ANGLESEY

Next page. As impressive as Plas Newydd is, its most striking feature is its setting above the Menai Strait, with views to Snowdonia beyond. Though there's been a house here since medieval times, its history as a 'stately home' really only dates from 1815, when owner Henry William Paget was made Marquess of Anglesey, in recognition of his heroism at Waterloo. The leg he lost in that field of glory was for many decades publicly displayed in Belgium; visitors to Plas Newydd today have to make do with a commemorative column in the grounds.

Beaumaris Castle
BEAUMARIS, ANGLESEY

Right. If Wales' cultural inheritance has been complex, so too has England's. Edward I, the 'Hammer of the Scots' and conquering nemesis of Wales' patriotic princes, is popularly (and understandably) viewed as an 'English' king. Yet this Plantagenet monarch was Anglo-Norman with close familial ties to the Loire Valley and other parts of northern France. We're reminded of this in the name his French-speaking engineers gave to the great castle they were charged with constructing in these *beaux barais* – or 'beautiful marshes' – by the Menai Strait.

The Dingle Nature Reserve
LLANGEFNI, ANGLESEY

Next page. Tricks of technology and nature go together to enchanting effect in this exquisite study of the River Cefni. The photographer's extended exposure doesn't just capture the crystal clarity of the stream and the tumbling energy of the rapids, but also the verdant eeriness of a scene illuminated by sunbeams filtered through the foliage of summer. Visible in the background, a boardwalk along the bank allows visitors to follow the river down the valley through ancient woodland for some distance, enjoying the beauty and tranquillity of this enchanting glen.

South Stack Lighthouse

HOLY ISLAND, ANGLESEY

Right. Lit up in a burst of pinks and oranges as the sun sets slowly over the Irish Sea, this famous lighthouse has 60-metre (197-foot) cliffs as its pedestal. The first plan to place some sort of beacon here as a warning to shipping on this most hazardous of coasts was drawn up in the 1660s, though the first lighthouse wasn't actually built until 1800. Separated from the shores of Holy Island by a deep and turbulent channel, the South Stack was difficult both to reach and to supply. Since 1984, the lighthouse has been unmanned.

Llanddwyn Island

NEWBOROUGH, ANGLESEY

Next page. Dramatically situated on a rocky outcrop at the western end of the Menai Strait, the lighthouse here was built in 1873. But Llanddwyn had by that time already been celebrated for centuries as the home of St Dwynwen, Wales' patron saint of lovers. (The ruins of her church on the island may still – just about – be seen.) Those who make the pilgrimage here today tend to be drawn more by the scenery of this achingly pretty tidal island which – small as it is – offer ssome of Wales' finest walks.

Llandudno
CONWY

Right. With the summits of Snowdonia brooding in the background, Llandudno's sweeping seafront gleams beneath the late-afternoon sun, its pale façades picking up the whites and greys of an atmospheric cloudscape. Founded in the 1820s on reclaimed coastal marshes, this handsome seaside resort was developed by the Liverpool architect Owen Williams with the co-operation of local landowner Lord Mostyn. Soon trains and paddle steamers were bringing holidaymakers and trippers from the industrial towns of northern England to what is still regarded as the 'Queen of Welsh Resorts'.

The Great Orme
LLANDUDNO, CONWY

Next page. This limestone headland outside Llandudno can be seen from far out at sea – hence its name. In Norse rather than Welsh, an *urm* was a mythological sea serpent, whose head this promontory seemed to resemble when seen from a distance. Long before the Viking age, though, the Great Orme was inhabited by humans; there is evidence of copper-mining dating back to Neolithic times. Now a nature reserve, rich in flora and fauna, it's also a haven of peace and quiet, a place to escape from the bustling life of Llandudno just below.

Conwy Castle
CONWY TOWN, CONWY

Right. Even now it has an intimidating air, so it's easy to imagine how formidable Conwy Castle must have looked to the Welsh inhabitants of the area in the 1280s. Conversely, though, this massive structure represents an implicit acknowledgement of English insecurity in what was still seen as hostile territory, the forbidding exterior concealing fear. With its solid central keep surrounded by an outer curtain wall, both seen here, Conwy Castle was a serious bit of military engineering. But this was just the start: the whole town of Conwy was protected by defensive walls.

Bodnant Garden
TAL-Y-CAFN, CONWY

Next page. Bodnant House, beside the River Conwy, is the home of the Aberconway family. Its grounds were given to the National Trust after the Second World War. They have become one of the most popular visitor attractions in North Wales. Laid out in the 1870s, these beautifully managed gardens cover over 39 hectares (96 acres), and include both formal and 'wilder' woodland sections of the sort shown here. Important as it is as a centre for botany, breeding and research, Bodnant is first and foremost one of the loveliest gardens in the world.

Dolwyddelan Castle
DOLWYDDELAN, CONWY

Right. Small, squat and somewhat unprepossessing in comparison with some of North Wales' more extensive and elaborate castles, Dolwyddelan nevertheless has a certain indefinable romantic ruggedness. It's partly the wildness of its setting; partly the stark simplicity of a construction that seems to mean business; partly too the historical symbolism of a stronghold which, originally built in the early thirteenth century for Prince Llywelyn the Great, was subsequently taken over and extended by England's Edward I. North Wales' whole history is encapsulated in architecture.

Llanrwst
CONWY

Next page. A symphony of yellows, browns, reds and russets, this autumn scene can hardly have changed since 1636 when local landowner Sir John Gwynn built the Pont Fawr across the rushing waters of the River Conwy. The Tu Hwynt i'r Bont, the beautiful little courthouse in the background, was already old by then, built in the fifteenth century. A popular base for climbers and walkers wishing to explore Snowdonia's mountains, Llanrwst lies in more forgiving, undulating country. The burial place of Prince Llywelyn the Great, who died in 1240, it has been a significant market centre for a thousand years.

The Fairy Glen
BETWS-Y-COED, CONWY

Right. The idea that this little valley is a 'fairy glen' may owe more to the Victorian tourist industry than to any real folk tradition (and still less to any actual supernatural presence), but it's a pardonable flight of fancy even so. How, without appeals to another dimension, do we account for the sense of wonder we feel in a place like this, with a roof of verdant branches; with a floor of foaming water; walled in by the sound of the rushing stream? How else do we explain our exquisite sense of being transported far away from the world outside?

Caernarfon Castle
CAERNARFON, GWYNEDD

Next page. The Normans had built a castle in Caernarfon by the end of the eleventh century, but that was an improvised affair of earth and timber. The majestic monument we see today was constructed on the orders of Edward I in the 1280s to secure his victory over Wales' rebellious princes. The scale of the undertaking is truly awe-inspiring, this magnificent castle merely the citadel for a whole town that was surrounded by protective walls. This view reminds us that access would for the most part have been by sea.

Penrhyn Castle
LLANDEGAI, GWYNEDD

Right. As if this part of Wales didn't already have enough castles, local landowner George Hay Dawkins-Pennant decided that it needed another in the early nineteenth century. This, the golden age of the 'Gothic' romance – all ghosts and horrors – was also the heyday of the architectural 'folly', and the two sensibilities met in this imitation Norman castle, dark and drear. Yet there is a precedent to Penrhyn; the manor house atop whose foundations the present 'castle' is built had been equipped with crenellated fortifications in the fifteenth century.

Dolbadarn Castle
LLANBERIS, GWYNEDD

Next page. Dolbadarn Castle commands the uphill approach to the Llanberis Pass through the rugged heart of Snowdonia. It was built by Prince Llywelyn the Great in the early thirteenth century. Though small and simple in comparison with the more famous constructions of Edward I (who captured this castle in 1283), its mountain setting gives it a special bleak and windswept charm, which appealed to eighteenth-century painters with their taste for the 'sublime'. This particular photo is taken from almost exactly the same perspective as that depicted by J.M.W. Turner in a famous painting of 1802.

The Ugly House
CAPEL CURIG, GWYNEDD

Right. Ty Hyll, 'the Ugly House', is said to have been built in the course of a single night in the fifteenth century, by a pair of opportunistic brothers. The law as it then stood – or so the story goes – said that if a complete house could be constructed on an area of common land between sundown one day and dawn the next, then those who built it could claim freehold on that land. That this tradition existed isn't in doubt; whether the Ugly House (the nickname is somewhat harsh) is really an example of it is more questionable.

The Snowdon Horseshoe
GWYNEDD

Next page. Just a few hours away from some of Britain's biggest cities, Snowdonia is a wonderful little wilderness. Mount Snowdon, naturally enough, is at its heart. What we think of as one mountain, though, is really a compact group of connected mountains: Yr Wyddfa, the highest, is flanked by others like Y Lliwedd and Crib Goch. Between them stretches the Horseshoe, one of Britain's most spectacular ridge-walks. An enjoyable scramble in the summer, this can become a real mountaineering challenge in the winter months – but it's a rewarding experience at any time of year.

The Snowdon Mountain Railway
GWYNEDD

Right. If Snowdon, as the outdoors purists complain, is really 'Britain's busiest mountain', then it's only fitting that it should have its own commuter line. The Snowdon Mountain Railway has been running for well over a century now; its trains have been covering the 7.5-kilometre (4.7-mile) route from Llanberis to the summit since 1896. Both steam and diesel locomotives are used, but, for safety on these steep inclines, the trains are 'pushed' instead of 'pulled', and every carriage is equipped with its own rack-and-pinion braking system.

The Sygun Copper Mine
BEDDGELERT, GWYNEDD

Next page. Snowdonia's depths can be as appealing as its heights. The immense geological forces that formed these mountains so many million centuries ago left behind a complex and fascinating mineral legacy. Humanity has of course been a comparative newcomer to North Wales, but it's thought that there's been mining here since Roman times. The Sygun Copper Mine began operations in the 1820s but was closed down by 1903; copper was being extracted more economically elsewhere, in the United States, Mexico and, most notably, Chile. It was reopened as a tourist attraction in the 1980s.

Llŷn Peninsula
GWYNEDD

Right. The rising sun cloaks the village of Morfa Nefyn in a mystic light: houses, beach and mountains emerge from the retreating gloom as though the world is waking up out of a dream. Who would guess that, in an hour or two, this will be an attractive but ordinary fishing village? Remarkable as they already are, the natural beauties of Northwest Wales are enhanced by the associations of druidic magic and of bardic poetry we bring with us. There's an atmospheric eeriness to these places, especially at the start and close of day.

Bardsey Island
GWYNEDD

Next page. Iona, Lindisfarne, Inishmore … many offshore islands around British coasts have had their sacred associations. Monastic communities favoured such isolated spots for their peace and their freedom from distractions in centuries gone by. For sheer holiness, however, none can surely compete with Bardsey Island, just over 3 kilometres (2 miles) off the tip of the Llŷn Peninsula, beneath whose turf no fewer than 20,000 saints are said to lie buried. Of the ancient monastery, only ruins now remain on an island given over to wildlife (it's a national nature reserve) and to sheep.

Ffestiniog Railway
PORTHMADOG, GWYNEDD

Right. Built to carry slate from the mines at Blaunau Ffestiniog to the coast at Porthmadog, the Ffestiniog Railway opened in 1836. With a narrow gauge (of 59.7 centimetres or 23.5 inches) allowing for the winding twists and turns of its mountain sections, it ran for 110 years before it was closed. Within a few years, however, bands of enthusiasts were hard at work attempting to reopen the railway. By the mid-1950s a partial service had been restored. No longer was it hauling slate, of course; since 1982, when it became fully operational again, over 200,000 tourists have ridden on it every year.

Portmeirion
GWYNEDD

Next page. It was in the 1920s that Sir Bertram Clough Williams-Ellis, who had earlier inherited the nearby house, Plas Brodanw, from his father, embarked upon what might be seen as one of the most whimsical design-projects of all time. Over the fifty years that followed, he set about transforming a Welsh village into an extravagantly stylized Italian town – all columned porticos, stuccoed façades and rococo swirls. Whether we see it as a playful folly or as a serious riposte to the sterilities of modernism, it's definitely one of the stranger sights awaiting the visitor to Wales.

Harlech Castle
HARLECH, GWYNEDD

Right. Harlech is perhaps the most convincingly warlike-looking of Edward I's Welsh castles. Standing in a naturally fortified position atop a rocky spur, with its squat, square shape and its massive gatehouse, it has an air of meaning business. The castle did indeed see a good deal of action not only during Edward's time but also after. Owain Glyndwr captured it in 1404 and made it the headquarters for his Welsh Revolt against Henry IV. It was in the thick of things again during the Wars of the Roses, and it became a Royalist stronghold in the English Civil War.

Shell Island
LLANBEDR, GWYNEDD

Next page. Morfa, also known as Shell Island, is not in fact an island but a peninsula – and wouldn't even be that had George Finch not diverted the course of the River Artro at its estuary 200 years ago. The enterprising Earl of Winchelsea hoped to improve the flow of water past his slate-wharves at Pensarn. He certainly succeeded in changing the nature of this bit of coast. So called for the shells heaped up each year by winter storms, Shell Island is a wonderfully remote-feeling scrap of coastal wilderness, a favourite for those who enjoy 'wild' camping.

Bala Lake (Llyn Tegid)
GWYNEDD

Right. Looking across the mirror-smooth water to the distant peak of Aran Benllyn, the jetty in the foreground an invitation to explore, we could hardly feel further removed from the world of industry and trade – but in North Wales as elsewhere in Britain, humankind and nature are more closely connected than we might think. Thomas Telford raised the level of the lake when, in the 1790s, he turned it into what amounted to a cistern with sluices to regulate the flow of the River Dee, which in its turn supplied his Ellesmere Canal with water.

Cadair Idris and Llynnau Cregennen
GWYNEDD

Next page. The name of this famous mountain, which rises to 890 metres (2,930 feet), has traditionally been translated as 'Chair of Idris' – Idris being some sketchily imagined giant or king of mythological antiquity, who liked to sit here, leaning back in his seat to watch the stars. Here, the rugged beauty of the mountain is set off by the sight of one of the Llynnau Cregennen (Cregennen Lakes) in the foreground. Though all too often overlooked in favour of the more famous sights of Snowdonia, this is one of the loveliest parts of Wales.

Northeast Wales

South of the Dee Estuary, the Welsh border runs through some of Britain's greenest, gentlest countryside. Further west, in Snowdonia, jagged peaks, rugged gorges and rushing streams announce a dramatic and wild landscape.

By contrast, Northeast Wales displays softer charms. Flintshire, for all the hardness its name might suggest, could hardly be more welcoming, with its undulating contours, its winding rivers and its wooded slopes. Denbighshire, though hillier, is never remotely mountainous, but has beauties of its own that those dashing through to experience the great outdoors to the west all too often ignore. But then it's always been this region's fate to be

caught betwixt and between one country and another. The present plight of the area (to the south of Flintshire), which languishes under the label 'The County Borough of Wrexham', reflects the difficulty of encapsulating what was always a threshold-territory. Another name for the area, the Marches – which is applied to an even more ambiguous region including those parts of the English counties that lie along the border with Wales – reminds us that an ambiguity in status has existed all the way down this border since medieval times. And yet the boundary between the two countries to this day remains very much as it did when King Offa built his dyke.

Rhyl
DENBIGHSHIRE

Right. Boats line up to await the returning tides in the Clwyd Estuary; behind them loom the structures of a modern amusement park. For most modern visitors, though, Rhyl's former function as a fishing village remains firmly in the background. The town has been a busy seaside resort since the 1830s. Like other British destinations, Rhyl has in recent decades struggled to compete with rivals resorts in the Mediterranean and beyond, and has relied on EU-funded regeneration schemes. Things are looking up, though with the whole seafront having been refurbished in the last few years.

Bodelwyddan Castle
RHYL, DENBIGHSHIRE

Next page. As imposing as it seems, Bodelwyddan is not so much a castle as a confection, the Victorian reconstruction of a fifteenth-century manor house. But its severest critics couldn't accuse its developer Sir John Hay Williams, a lead-mining mogul, of a lack of eccentric vision; or its architects (Joseph Hansom and Edmund Welch) of lacking imagination or enterprise. The nearest it came to seeing military action was during the First World War, when wounded soldiers were treated within whilst able-bodied comrades trained in trench-warfare in the grounds.

Denbigh Castle
DENBIGH, DENBIGHSHIRE

Right. Edward I built this castle and fortified the town below in the 1280s, as a bastion of English civilization (or, at any rate, of obedience to the English Crown). The Welsh had other ideas. As early as 1294, a band of rebels led by Prince Madog ap Llywelyn had taken the castle by storm and remained in occupation for a year. Retaken by the English, the castle was better defended in 1400 when a force led by the charismatic Owain Glyndwr (*c.* 1349/59–*c.* 1415) – in revolt against King Henry IV – failed to take it after a siege.

The Offa's Dyke Path
CLWYDIAN HILLS, DENBIGHSHIRE

Next page. The Anglo-Saxon answer to Hadrian's Wall, Offa's Dyke ran for anything up to 240 kilometres (150 miles) between the mouths of the Severn and the Dee. King Offa of Mercia (who reigned from 757 to 796) built this earthen rampart all the way up his western border, both to exclude the Welsh and to impress his English subjects with his wealth and strength. Today it's the route of a footpath whose popularity isn't difficult to understand when you see the sort of scenery on offer from this northern section, in the Clwydian Hills of Denbighshire.

Moel Famau
CLWYDIAN HILLS, DENBIGHSHIRE

Right. Running north–south down Denbighshire's eastern edge, the Clwydian Hills are a mountain range in miniature. Moel Famau, the highest peak, rises to a height of only 555 metres (1,820 feet). What they lack in outright altitude, however, they more than make up for in wild charm, with all the ruggedness of mountains twice their height and views as beautiful as any to be found in the Scottish Highlands; or, for that matter, among the peaks of Snowdonia, in favour of which the treasures of eastern Wales are so often overlooked.

Llangollen
DENBIGHSHIRE

Next page. It was in the seventh century that St Collen set up a little church on the banks of the Dee, hence the name of the resulting town: Llangollen means 'Church of Collen'. The river, which rushes over rapids here, was bridged for the first time in the fourteenth century, though the medieval structure has been rebuilt and widened since. Today, Llangollen is famous as the centre for the International Eisteddfod, an annual celebration of music, dance and culture. Eisteddfods were a Welsh tradition: the International Eisteddfod, first held in 1943, brought the best of the world's culture home to Wales.

Plas Newydd
LLANGOLLEN, DENBIGHSHIRE

Right. The Ladies of Llangollen, Sarah Ponsonby and Eleanor Butler, were one of the more curious cultural phenomena of early nineteenth-century Britain. Both were daughters of the Anglo-Irish aristocracy, intended by their families for advantageous marriages. Instead, they chose to run away and live together, setting up home in this attractive house, which they beautified in the Gothic style. Formidably intellectual, they attracted a steady stream of visitors: poets like Sir Walter Scott, Wordsworth, Shelley, Byron, the philanthropist Josiah Wedgwood – and even the Duke of Wellington – made the pilgrimage to see them here.

View from Castell Dinas Brân
LLANGOLLEN, DENBIGHSHIRE

Next page. Walkers come up here today to enjoy uninterrupted views across miles of open country in all directions. In centuries past, though, these stunning views were strategically significant. Hence the siting here, not only of the castle for which the hill is named but also of a prehistoric hill fort, built in about 600 BC. The Clwydian Hills have proven rich in Iron Age remains; many sites have been identified, including several hill forts with banked-earth ramparts such as those on Moel Arthur, Penycloddiau and Foel Fenlli further north.

Lighthouse at Talacre Beach
PRESTATYN, FLINTSHIRE

Right. There's been a lighthouse here since 1776, unusual as it is to find one placed directly upon the beach, marking the Point of Ayr and the western entrance to the Dee Estuary. The present building dates from the 1820s; its predecessor was destroyed by a succession of storms. Now this one has been abandoned, rendered redundant by modern satellite navigation-systems, but the tower still stands, an isolated and increasingly unsettling presence. In the lowering light of sunset, it can seem to 'float' above the water. Inevitably, there have been claims that it is haunted.

Pontcysyllte Aqueduct
CEFN MAWR, COUNTY BOROUGH OF WREXHAM

Next page. The engineers Thomas Telford and William Jessop built this aqueduct in 1805 to carry the Llangollen Canal across the valley of the River Dee. The construction method of Telford's own invention was unusual. Basically, the water sits in a long, cast-iron trough which is held up by hollow pillars built of brick. Many at the time were sceptical, but the resulting aqueduct was not only admirably functional, it was also elegant and shapely. Even today, long after the canal was closed, it remains one of the most beautiful monuments we have to the Industrial Revolution.

Chirk Castle and Gardens

CHIRK, COUNTY BOROUGH OF WREXHAM

Right. Edward I built Chirk Castle at the end of the thirteenth century. A link in the chain of fortresses he founded for the subjugation of North Wales, Chirk made the transition to peacetime more successfully than the others. By the beginning of the seventeenth century it was more a fortified stately home than a castle, with stunning staterooms and galleries and a handsome library; its grounds were beautifully landscaped in the eighteenth century. Even so, seen from certain angles it can look as uncompromisingly warlike as it ever did, a striking emblem of military power.

Erddig Hall

WREXHAM, COUNTY BOROUGH OF WREXHAM

Next page. Dating from the 1680s, when it was built for the then High Sheriff of Denbighshire, Joshua Edisbury, Erddig has been very handsomely preserved. The house was extended in the eighteenth century, when the grounds were also extensively and ambitiously landscaped; further improvements were made in the Victorian era. In the age of *Downton Abbey*, it's proven particularly popular with tourists for the insights it offers into the experiences of those servants and staff who looked after the house's wealthy owners. Erddig's National Trust curators have placed special emphasis on the life that was lived here 'below stairs'.

Mid Wales

Wales as a whole, as this book shows, abounds in 'undiscovered' beauties, but a great deal of its central section has been more or less ignored.

Not without good reason: the Cambrian Mountains may not be as spectacular as those of Snowdonia (their highest peak Plumlumon, or Plynlimon, rises to only 752 metres/2,467 feet) but the area still has an uncompromisingly upland feel. Even in the nineteenth century, travellers knew this central region as the 'Green Desert' of Wales – lush and fertile, but undeveloped, and to a considerable extent unpeopled. To this day there are few settlements

of any size, whilst large areas remain unreached by any road. Yet it's well worth the effort of exploring what amounts to a secret wilderness within just a short drive of some of Britain's biggest cities. Paradoxically, the more obviously rugged Brecon Beacons to the south have tended to attract more visitors whilst the Cambrian Mountains have remained unknown – a pity, because they are every bit as beautiful; and in some ways easier to explore. The coast as well has proven popular since the coming of the railways in the nineteenth century opened the way to the development of resorts like Aberystwyth and Aberaeron.

Aberystwyth
CEREDIGION

Right. 'Place of learning, place of water, place of sky', wrote Ian McMillan of Aberystwyth, at whose famous university he'd spent a fulfilling year as poet-in-residence. He is by no means the only Aber-enthusiast: in November 2014, Aberystwyth was officially awarded the Academy of Urbanism's 'Great Town' title. But the Victorian resort, which became an academic centre, arguably has an unfair advantage in its location beside the Irish Sea, and boasts one of the most magnificent promenades in the British Isles.

Aberaeron
CEREDIGION

Next page. Yachts rest on the muddy floor of Aberaeron harbour at low tide, in the glimmer of the evening. Handsome houses line the quayside in the background. This attractive little resort was to a quite extraordinary extent the conception of one man: a local cleric, the Reverend Alban Thomas-Jones Gwynne. Seeing the potential of the place, he had a special Act of Parliament passed allowing him to rebuild and enlarge Aberaeron's harbour at his own expense. He envisaged a commercial port and shipbuilding centre, but the new Aberaeron instead became the perfect haven for pleasure craft.

Devil's Bridge Falls
NEAR ABERYSTWYTH, CEREDIGION

Right. The River Rheidol plunges 90 metres (almost 300 feet) here, down a deep and narrow gorge over a series of waterfalls. It is so difficult a crossing, it took the Devil to build a bridge, or so the story goes. In reality the story is quite different, for the village has boasted not just one bridge but three, each piggy-backing on its predecessor. The oldest, built at the beginning of the twelfth century, provided a platform for the workers erecting a second stone bridge in 1753. This formed the foundation of the modern iron-constructed bridge.

Bwlch Nant yr Arian Forest Park
PONTERWYD, CEREDIGION

Next page. At the heart of Mid Wales is that wild and empty plateau known as the Elenydd. Its more prosaic English name, the Cambrian Mountains, barely does it justice. Long dismissed as the 'Green Desert' of Wales, it's actually anything but arid, though it's among Britain's most sparsely populated regions. This view, across the Bwlch Nant yr Arian Forest Park, is typical: stands of trees punctuate miles of rugged hills, boggy hollows and open moorland. Red kites spiral in these endless skies; the peregrine falcon flies free. The sense of tranquillity has to be experienced to be believed.

New Quay
CEREDIGION

Right. A seagull stands sentinel on a rock outside the entrance to the harbour at New Quay, one of the most appealing little towns to be found on Ceredigion's charming coast. Still a working fishing port, it's also an attractive holiday resort – small in size, picturesque in its architecture and with both sandy and shingle beaches. Ideally suited to watersports, it's also the ideal base for sailing out in Cardigan Bay, as well as for making forays inland into the wilds of the Elenydd and beyond.

The Beach at Mwnt
CEREDIGION

Next page. Development along this stretch of the Ceredigion coast has been strictly controlled by the National Trust, hence the unspoiled appeal of this sandy beach and the ravishing beauty of its hinterland; this despite the fact that the 'undiscovered' attractions of the place have been widely promoted of late, bringing crowds of visitors all summer long. The clifftop church above the beach dates from the fourteenth century, though the font inside is even older and may well have been present when the village was attacked by Flemish invaders on Mwnt's Red Sunday at the beginning of January 1155.

Cardigan Island from Poppit Sands
CEREDIGION

Right. Looking out from the rocky shore we see a distant prospect of Cardigan Island – not much more than a silhouette sandwiched between a misty sea and a lilac sky. Standing some 200 metres (220 yards) out from the mainland coast of Ceredigion in the Teifi Estuary, Cardigan Island is uninhabited; except, that is, for a wealth of wildlife, including a colony of seals and nesting flocks of fulmars, guillemots, razorbills, cormorants, shags and gulls. Bottlenose dolphins – one of the great attractions of Cardigan Bay for nature-loving tourists – regularly patrol the waters just offshore.

Powis Castle
WELSHPOOL, POWYS

Next page. In 1286, reading the writing on the wall after the defeat of his neighbours to the north, Owain ap Gruffydd ap Gwenwynwyn, Prince of Powys, came to terms with Edward I of England. Hence the Welsh prince's reinvention as a quasi-Norman, 'Baron de la Pole', or in other words the lord of what was now called Welshpool. The better part of valour, this discretion certainly saved the fabric of Powis Castle which still stands today – and has been much improved over the centuries – as one of Britain's finest stately homes.

Craig Goch
ELAN VALLEY, POWYS

Right. It's well known that South Wales had an important role in the Industrial Revolution. But there's a whole history to be written of the part played – more discreetly – by rural Wales. The northern landscape, as we have seen, is marked by Telford's railway bridges (*see* page 20) and aqueducts (*see* page 96), but the face of Mid Wales too was subtly (and not-so subtly) changed. The Elan Valley was transformed by the construction of a series of reservoirs in the Victorian Age, all so that the City of Birmingham could continue to expand.

Brecon
POWYS

Next page. This delightful little market town lies just inside the Brecon Beacons National Park, which has helped preserve its historic character. Its history predates the coming of the Normans by a millennium at least. The Romans had a fort at the crossing of the River Usk, whilst today's town of Brecon may well take its name from that of Brychon, a semi-mythic hero of Irish birth who established a kingdom here in Celtic times. Today, the epic note may be absent, but the place's picturesque appeal is everywhere.

The Brecon Beacons from Pen y Fan

POWYS

Right. Standing 886 metres (2,907 feet) above sea level, the summit of Pen y Fan affords spectacular views over the other peaks, just slightly lower, of the Brecon Beacons. Here, looking eastward along a jagged ridge, we see the peak of Cribyn (795 metres or 2,600 feet) and beyond it many miles of open moorland grazed by sheep and Welsh ponies. One of Britain's most beautiful wildernesses, the Brecon Beacons are a paradise for walkers and outdoor enthusiasts of every kind. The area was awarded national park status in 1957.

Sgwd y Pannwr Waterfall

BRECON BEACONS, POWYS

Next page. Between its meteorological character and its geological quirks, this part of Wales is rich in waterfalls, but few are quite so appealing as the Fullers' Falls on the Afon Mellte. Whether wool was actually washed (or 'fulled') in these waters in days gone by or this is just a colourful tradition is unclear. Either way, this is a wonderful place to sit and watch the torrent thundering down – especially when, as here, it's swollen by the melting snows of spring. If you tire of the sight, there are further cataracts upriver.

Hay-on-Wye
POWYS

Right. The first – and still by far the best known – of Britain's designated 'book towns', Hay hosts a famous literary festival at the beginning of June each year. Top authors (and their readers) flock here from every corner of the world for ten days of readings, signings, interviews and debates, and to browse in the many bookshops of the town. But there's more to the place than books. A lovely little market town, Hay has the remains of not one but two castles, both dating back to Norman times. It's the perfect centre for exploring the Wye Valley.

Llangorse Lake
BRECON BEACONS, POWYS

Next page. Wales' answer to Loch Ness, complete with *afanc*, or mythic monster, Llangorse Lake is 1.6 kilometres (a mile) long. It was left behind by retreating glaciers 15,000 years ago, and its environs may have been inhabited for a fair proportion of the time since then. There is evidence that agriculture was being practised here from approximately 4,000 BC – nomadic hunter-gatherer groups very likely came this way a long time before. At some point in the prehistoric period, a *crannog* (an artificial island, built by a prehistoric community as a secure home) was constructed near its northern shore.

West Wales

The Scottish Highlands, the Irish Gaeltacht, Cornwall, Brittany in France and Galicia in Spain; Europe's Celtic heartlands have always lain in its western margins.

The same might be said of Wales itself and its position in the British landmass, although not, paradoxically, within the country, whose most western-lying region has for the best part of a thousand years been known as a 'Little England'. Linguistically and culturally, the southern parts of Pembrokeshire and Carmarthenshire have been firmly English in their focus. The so-called 'landsker line', dividing the Welsh- and English-

speaking zones, runs right through the centre of Pembrokeshire, creating a division which has been as sharp as it is unaccountable. Anglo-Norman domination was a force here from early on. Henry I brought Flemish weavers here to develop the economy in the early twelfth century, but they seem to have been entirely assimilated within a hundred years or so. Why their presence should have made the place more 'English' isn't clear. Industrial Swansea excepted, this part of the country has not been as obviously urbanized as others. This is without doubt one of Wales' loveliest and least spoiled regions.

Cenarth Falls

CENARTH, PEMBROKESHIRE

Right. Every autumn, the salmon and seatrout return to the Teifi and, swimming upriver, find this formidable obstacle in their way. What follows is one of nature's great performances as the migratory fish are forced to battle their way up the Cenarth Falls. Leaping forward, falling back, summoning all their strength and trying, again and again, until, finally successful, they forge on to their breeding grounds upstream. The salmon fishery has been vital to the Cenarth economy for centuries, and traditional hide-covered basket boats or 'coracles' are still used.

Poppit Sands

ST DOGMAELS, PEMBROKESHIRE

Next page. Backed by undulating dunes, this spacious sandy beach lies alongside the Teifi Estuary. It's a favourite spot for swimming, surfing, or just lazing in the sun. In the winter it attracts anglers who come here to catch an extensive range of fish. This aspect of the beach's appeal has been known for centuries: aerial photography from 2009 found a V-shaped wall of rocks over 250 metres (280 yards) long just a little way offshore. Archaeologists have identified this as a fish-trap built in Norman times, designed to corral fish for netting as the tide retreated.

Pentre Ifan Dolmen
PRESELI HILLS, PEMBROKESHIRE

Right. Once, it's thought, this structure would have provided the portal for a mound within which some important prehistoric chieftain lay interred. The earth has long since been worn away, leaving this freestanding collection of five stones. The largest of these weighs anything up to 17 tonnes, yet it seems almost to float here, poised, on the points of its three supports, a miracle of Stone-Age engineering. Other stones in the vicinity (including some recently unearthed by archaeologists) suggest that this was a major burial complex, dating back to about 3,500 BC.

Stack Rocks
ST GOVAN'S HEAD, PEMBROKESHIRE

Next page. With its dizzying cliffs, rocky islets, secluded inlets and sandy beaches, the Pembrokeshire coast is a walker's paradise. A national park since 1952, it's been marked out as a long-distance footpath since 1970. Twin pillars, now standing in splendid isolation, Stack Rocks were once the supports for limestone arches hollowed out by the action of the waves over countless centuries. A nesting site in spring to the guillemots from which they take their name in Welsh (*Elegug*), Stack Rocks are among the many scenic glories of this coast.

St David's Cathedral
ST DAVID'S, PEMBROKESHIRE

Right. If city status is to be determined (as it traditionally has been) by the presence of a cathedral, then St David's is Britain's smallest city. There *is* a cathedral here – and a very handsome one, dating from the twelfth century – even if there's very little else. Currently hovering around the 2,000 mark, the population here has never been much more than that, nor does this miniature metropolis boast much more than a dozen little streets. It's important emblematically, though: the cathedral houses St David's tomb – this sixth-century bishop is of course the patron saint of Wales.

Lily Ponds, Stackpole Estate
BOSHERSTON, PEMBROKESHIRE

Next page. Stackpole is an anomaly: conceived and created as the estate for a stately home, it was left bereft by the abandonment of Stackpole Court in the 1940s. Its actual demolition in 1963 left the estate orphaned twice over. Since then it's been a grounds without a house. Not that this has fazed the National Trust, or the visitors in their thousands who come each year to enjoy its 12 square kilometres (4.5 square miles) of woods and parkland, rocky cliffs, sandy beaches and man-made lakes such as this one.

Whitesands Bay and Ramsey Island

ST DAVID'S HEAD, PEMBROKESHIRE

Right. Looking down from the rocky Carn Llidi, just to the northeast, we see the glowing sands of one of Wales' finest beaches set off by the dazzling white of the surf and the jewelled azure of the sea. Beyond the bay lies Ramsey Island, of international importance as a wildlife refuge, particularly rich in seal and seabird colonies. This part of the Pembrokeshire coast shows signs of human habitation back to the Bronze Age and beyond. More recently, St Patrick is said to have set out from here to undertake his mission to Ireland in the fifth century.

Tenby Harbour

PEMBROKESHIRE

Next page. Though Castle Hill, seen in the background here, still dominates the scene, not too much of Tenby's medieval fortress remains. The old town walls are another story, remaining in remarkably good repair, especially the fortified Five Arches gatehouse. The modern resort developed inland of the old town and around the north and western sides of the harbour. Local magnate Sir William Paxton did much to develop the new resort: in 1814 he built a road supported by seventeen arches with stunning sea views, known as 'Paxton's Promenade'.

Carew Castle
CAREW, PEMBROKESHIRE

Right. This has long been a strategic site, at the mouth of Milford Haven. The remains of an Iron Age fort have been discovered, and there's been a castle here since the eleventh century. The present one, built in 1270 but much-modified thereafter, was for generations the home of the Carew family. It kept its name, despite being taken over by Rhys ap Thomas, a friend of Tudor founder (and Pembroke native) Henry VII in the fifteenth century. After changing hands again a number of times, it fell into decay from the eighteenth century, though it has been partially restored in recent years.

Llyn y Fan Fach, Black Mountain
CARMARTHENSHIRE

Next page. The Black Mountain isn't a mountain as such, but a range in its own right. Despite its name, it shouldn't be confused with the Black Mountains, further to the east. Nor is it truly to be associated with the Brecon Beacons, though it lies at the western edge of the Brecon Beacons National Park. Yet there's no doubt or ambiguity about the area's beauty, or the eerie atmosphere of quiet. It's no surprise to find that this little lake has otherworldly associations: legend has it that a fairy woman once emerged from these waters to wed a local man.

View from the Sugarloaf
LLANWRTYD WELLS, CARMARTHENSHIRE

Right. The 'sugarloaf' hasn't been in common domestic use for upward of a hundred years, so it's hard for us to understand its ubiquity as a topographic term. There's at least one other 'sugarloaf' mountain in Wales alone (*see* page 236), others in Ireland and the United States, and, of course, the most famous of all in Rio de Janeiro in Brazil. The point about the sugarloaf *was* its point. It came as a cone of crystal sugar, bits of which were broken off for use as they were needed. The resemblance to this Carmarthenshire hill must once have been quite striking.

National Botanic Garden of Wales
LLANARTHNEY, CARMARTHENSHIRE

Next page. Sir William 'Tenby' Paxton bought Middleton Hall and its surrounding parkland in 1789 and promptly set about building an extravagant new hall and creating a sumptuous water park outside. An excess of patriotism after Lord Nelson's death at Trafalgar in 1805 prompted the building of a neo-Gothic tower. Under more sober management now as the National Botanic Garden, the place is as picturesque as ever, but also a world-class facility for serious research. Paxton's hall has been replaced, with fitting grandeur, by the biggest single-span glasshouse in the world.

Carreg Cennen Castle
LLANDEILO, CARMARTHENSHIRE

Right. A mass of medieval masonry, this castle has been a ruin for five hundred years, but its position atop a limestone escarpment makes it something more spectacular, sublime even. Built in the thirteenth and fourteenth centuries, it was fought over by the Welsh and English, in 1403 withstanding a siege of several months by Owain Glyndwr's rebel force. A Lancastrian stronghold during the Wars of the Roses, in 1461 it was captured by the Yorkists and partially demolished. The castle we see now was substantially renovated in the nineteenth century.

Dryslwyn Castle
LLANDEILO, CARMARTHENSHIRE

Next page. In the early thirteenth century the sons of Rhys ap Gruffydd (1132–97) were forced to fight for the little kingdom of Deheubarth over which their father had reigned. The brothers built this stronghold as a base from which they could wage their campaign. Soon, however, all Welsh squabbles were to be set aside in the face of a more formidable threat from the English. Edward I took Dryslwyn after a siege in 1287. It was captured by Owain Glyndwr in his revolt of 1403 and subsequently destroyed by the English to pre-empt further rebellions.

Kidwelly Castle
KIDWELLY, CARMARTHENSHIRE

Right. It's not every medieval castle that looks the part as much as Kidwelly does, so much so that it featured in the opening shot of the film *Monty Python and the Holy Grail* (1975). Standing majestically on a raised-up 'motte' or mound, it's additionally protected on one side by the River Gwendraeth. Inside, an open yard or 'bailey' is guarded by four massively built round towers. A strongly built gatehouse controls its entrance to the west. The castle was built in stages between the thirteenth and fifteenth centuries.

Pendine Sands
CARMARTHENSHIRE

Next page. Extending uninterrupted for upwards of 11 kilometres (7 miles) along the coast of Carmarthen Bay, this is one of the most beautiful beaches in the British Isles. In winter you can walk for hours and scarcely see a soul, but in the summer season, it becomes a busy playground; that is, when the military allows – for much of this coast belongs to the Ministry of Defence and is in use as a firing range – and when motor enthusiasts aren't attempting to set new speed records or to test hot-rod cars on what amounts to a natural racetrack.

Dylan Thomas' Shed
LAUGHARNE, CARMARTHENSHIRE

Right. When not raising hell in London and New York, the poet spent his last few years in Laugharne, which is generally believed to be the model for the little town in which the action of his classic verse-drama *Under Milk Wood* unfolds. There, notoriously, it's named Llareggub (Welsh-sounding, but actually 'Buggerall' backwards), a tragicomic community that runs on gossip, envy and unfulfilled yearning. Thomas actually wrote his play in New Quay (*see* page 116) to which the description is closer, but Llareggub is all about its people, and they were here.

Rhossili Bay
GOWER PENINSULA, SWANSEA

Next page. Just a stone's throw from the city of Swansea, but it might be the other end of the world, Rhossili Bay lies at the southwestern tip of the Gower Peninsula. As if straining out to sea for space, this natural projection into the Bristol Channel is a haven of beauty, peace and quiet, and of ravishing coastal scenery, including rugged cliffs and sandy beaches like this one. Gower was the first place in the United Kingdom to be awarded 'Area of Outstanding Natural Beauty' status, in 1949, allowing strict control to be exercised over development and exploitation.

Three Cliffs Bay
GOWER PENINSULA, SWANSEA

Right. These cliffs are clearly to be seen in this view from the land: the first in the far background; the second in the centre; the third to the right, this side of the mouth of the stream known as Pennard Pill. To all the usual seaside pursuits of sunbathing, swimming and surfing, may be added rock climbing – everything from casual scrambling (ironically, the tallest cliff is the easiest) to VS ('Very Severe'). Rare plants are to be found among the dunes inland, as well as Pennard Castle, a ruin dating from about the thirteenth century.

The Millennium Bridge
SWANSEA

Next page. Past and future meet in the Millennium Bridge, a triumph of twenty-first century technology and up-to-date design which takes the shape of a stylized sail – an apparently outmoded means of marine propulsion. But then in an eco-conscious age, all of us have to question the uncritical store we once set by a sort of 'progress' which was measured in ever newer, bigger, more energy-hungry systems. Swansea is leading the way towards a much more environmentally-sensitive future: this bridge, built for pedestrians and cyclists, is a declaration of intent.

Clyne Gardens
SWANSEA

Right. These beautiful botanical gardens were endowed in the 1860s by Richard Glynn Vivian. The heir to a massive mining fortune and a keen connoisseur and collector, Glynn Vivian is most famous as the founder of Swansea's city art museum. It was his nephew Algernon who shaped the gardens as we see them now. Extending over almost 20 hectares (47 acres), they are beautifully landscaped, laid out with (for example) an exquisitely ornamental Japanese garden, a bluebell wood and a special garden dedicated to the cultivation of bog-plants. The stands of oak trees have been here since Norman times.

Mumbles Pier
SWANSEA

Next page. While some might suggest Mumbles is no more than a suburb of Swansea, anyone who's spent time in this lively little resort knows how different it is in character and tone. Nestling against the headland of the same (peculiar) name, it marks the southwestern end of Swansea Bay, fronting the sea with an appealing promenade. Lined with attractive cafés and pubs, it's the perfect place for a summer stroll or a foray down to the beach for a paddle or a swim. Serious surfers venture round the promontory, with its two little islets, to Langland Bay.

South Wales

Their headwaters rising in the hills to the north, along the edge of what is now the Brecon Beacons National Park, a series of rivers runs roughly parallel down to the coastal plain and to the Bristol Channel.

Revealed by erosion over millions of years, coal seams were discovered close to the surface here and, as a result, from the eighteenth century, the Valleys became one of Britain's first and most important industrial regions. South Wales has been shaped by the opposing characters of the Valleys and the Vale of Glamorgan: where one area was industrialized, the other is largely open farmland. Even in the former, whilst men toiled in

darkness, dirt and danger below ground, lovely hillsides lay above. 'How Green Was My Valley', marvelled Richard Llywelyn in the title of his famous novel, which was destined to become a still more famous film.

The area's industrial heritage has been a bittersweet patrimony in these post-industrial times, leaving a legacy of unemployment, poverty and social problems. Even so, it's an important inheritance in which great pride is rightly taken. With exciting cities like Cardiff, stately homes, Roman ruins and some of Britain's most beautiful countryside, South Wales is ripe for rediscovery.

Afan Forest Park

NEATH PORT TALBOT

Right. Mountain bikers come from far and wide to ride the precipitous trails of Afan Forest Park, among the most enjoyably challenging – and beautiful – in the world. But there's plenty of scope for gentler fun. The less adventurous can explore a network of cycle-paths created along the paths of disused railway lines, the area's industrial heritage put to modern leisure use. There are tracks set aside for walkers too. Indeed, there's something for anyone who wants to blow away the cobwebs with a day outdoors, just a short drive from Neath or Bridgend.

Cyfarthfa Castle

CYFARTHFA PARK, MERTHYR TYDFIL COUNTY BOROUGH

Next page. This is Wales, and we aren't exactly short of castles. Cyfarthfa remains of interest, however, as testimony to the importance of industrialism in modern times. New – or newish – money built this pile, that of the Crawshays, descendants of the Yorkshire-born ironmaster Richard Crawshay (1739–1818) who had grown rich as owner of Merthyr Tydfil's Cyfarthfa works. Why the castellated walls and towers for what was never to be more than a luxurious dwelling? If it was good enough for Edward I and his feudal lords, it was good enough for the new overseers.

Cwmcarn Forest
CWMCARN, CAERPHILLY

Right. Walking these wooded hillsides in the bracing crispness of an autumn afternoon, it's easy to forget that we're in colliery country. For Cwmcarn is in the Ebbw Valley, famous for its pits in days gone by, and now an area struggling to find an economic function in modern, post-mining times. Hence, at least in part, the development of local attractions like the Cwmcarn Forest Drive (recently boosted by the opening of a new visitor centre; though temporarily closed due to infected larch trees). There are hopes that tourism may help to take the place of coal.

Caerphilly Castle
CAERPHILLY TOWN, CAERPHILLY

Next page. A youthful ally of the future Edward I, Gilbert de Clare, 7th Earl of Gloucester, was rewarded for his loyalty with the lordships of Abergavenny and Brecknock (now Brecon). Gifts of this kind allowed the King to police an unstable region through his feudal supporters. Gilbert made a perfect 'Marcher Lord', and he built Caerphilly Castle (1268–71) in the course of his conquest of Glamorgan (despite a setback when Llywelyn ap Gruffudd burned the partially built structure down). Today, with its massive walls and gatehouse and elaborate water-defences, it is one of Britain's most impressive castles.

Ironworkers' Cottages
BLAENAVON, TORFAEN

Right. This part of Wales was in the vanguard of the Industrial Revolution. Blaenavon Ironworks began operations in 1788. A group of entrepreneurs from the English Midlands had leased the site from Lord Abergavenny (there was a revolution too in the ways in which land was being owned and managed). Rich both in coal and iron ore, Blaenavon was crisscrossed with streams, sources for the water needed for the new steam-driven extraction methods. By 1845, over 35,000 tonnes of iron were being produced per year, though as the century wore on, more emphasis was placed on steel.

Ogmore Castle
NEAR OGMORE-BY-SEA, BRIDGEND COUNTY BOROUGH

Next page. Not too much is left of the twelfth-century castle here, but it certainly makes an atmospheric ruin. It stands on a strategic site on a little island made by the confluence of the Afon Ewenny with the River Ogmore. Its dilapidation if anything adds to its setting's stunning beauty. This Norman stronghold hasn't been an abandoned ruin as long as it would appear, and actually remained in use until the nineteenth century, at which time it was home to a courthouse and a gaol. It's no surprise to find that there have been persistent claims that the place is haunted.

Merthyr Mawr
BRIDGEND COUNTY BOROUGH

Next page. Merthyr Mawr House is handsome, built in the early nineteenth century in the Classical style. However, impressive as it may be, it is overshadowed architecturally by the cottages its owner (MP and Judge John Nicholls) built nearby for his employees. What is now called the village of Merthyr Mawr is quite exquisite: all picturesque thatched cottages amidst lovingly tended gardens. Further afield, though still in the grounds of the big house, are the remains of an Iron Age hill fort; this whole area is rich in archaeological finds.

Kenfig Pool National Nature Reserve
NEAR PORTHCAWL, BRIDGEND COUNTY BOROUGH

Next page. Sand dunes make for a dynamic landscape – always on the move, their contours ever shifting. Here, it's been suggested, they may actually have dammed and diverted the course of the River Kenfig, or of another nearby stream, creating the large freshwater pool which is at the centre of this wildlife sanctuary. Local legends of a lost city lying beneath its waters, whilst surely an exaggeration, belie the possibility that ancient settlements have indeed been drowned or buried under the landscape as it's changed over the centuries.

Porthcawl
BRIDGEND COUNTY BOROUGH

Right. Porthcawl's promenade was built in 1887 to mark the Golden Jubilee of Queen Victoria, but it also marked a shrewd appreciation of the economic realities of the time. This little town had come to local prominence as a port for exporting coal, but by the 1880s it was being overtaken in this regard by Barry, further east along the coast. So Porthcawl decided to reinvent itself as a resort. And very successful it was at that, until in recent decades it was hit by the double blow of a declining Welsh coalfield and the boom in foreign package holidays.

Dyffryn Gardens
COWBRIDGE, VALE OF GLAMORGAN

Next page. There's been a manor house here since as long ago as the seventh century, though the present-day Dyffryn House wasn't built until the 1890s. Owner John Cory was a coal exporter and ship owner from Barry. It was under his son, a keen horticulturalist, that the gardens here were developed into their present stunning state. Reginald Cory personally sponsored a series of expeditions to far-flung parts of the world in search of unknown species. The finds from these trips were to form the basis for the collection we see on show today.

Llantwit Major

VALE OF GLAMORGAN

Right. This little town beside the Bristol Channel takes its name from St Illtud, a famous teacher of the sixth century. The theological college he established here came to be known and respected the length and breadth of Christendom; as many as 2,000 scholars might have studied here at any one time. By the tenth century, though, a series of Viking raids had made monastic life much more difficult. Operations continued, but on a smaller scale. A thousand years later, though its academic heyday is a distant memory, the town of Llantwit still has a charming medieval feel.

Nash Point

MONKNASH, VALE OF GLAMORGAN

Next page. Jutting dramatically out into the Bristol Channel, this limestone headland overlooks a rocky shore (though there are beautiful sandy beaches immediately to the north). This whole section of coast near Monknash has been designated a Site of Special Scientific Interest, but it is of considerable scenic interest too. Along with fresh air and exercise, walkers along these clifftops can expect a variety of stunning views. Whether one pushes north towards Porthcawl or turns south in the direction of Llantwit Major, it's a hugely rewarding experience either way.

Porthkerry Country Park
BARRY, VALE OF GLAMORGAN

Right. For decades, daily trains carried coal across this viaduct to the nearby port of Barry for export around the world. But Barry had reached its height as a coal port by the beginning of the First World War. For the rest of the twentieth century, it was a story of slow decline, though even now the viaduct remains in use. Still, Porthkerry Country Park, with its wooded valleys, its fields and its little shingle beach, offers a welcome escape into nature for the nearby communities of Porthkerry and of Barry.

Jackson's Bay, Barry Island
VALE OF GLAMORGAN

Next page. The construction of the coal docks at Barry made what had been a tidal island into a peninsula, and facilitated its development as a resort. If the sandy beach at Jackson's Bay has been there since time immemorial, the Barry Island Pleasure Park nearby is hardly new: it opened its gates for the first time as long ago as 1897. Sadly, they were closed again for good in 2014, after several tricky years, and now the complex awaits demolition and redevelopment. But the beach seems set to go on and on.

Cosmeston Lakes Country Park
PENARTH, VALE OF GLAMORGAN

Right. This lovely park has been created in what was once a limestone-quarrying complex, which closed in 1969 after being worked for almost a hundred years. Two excavations were turned into lakes, whilst others were filled in and landscaped to create a country park with a variety of different habitats, including woodland, wetland, meadow and open grassland. In the course of landscaping, workers stumbled on the remains of a fourteenth-century village. This has now been painstakingly restored as an educational project, and has also provided a playground for medieval battle re-enactors.

Wales Millennium Centre
CARDIFF

Next page. 'In these stones horizons sing', says the English script, fittingly enough for what is primarily a concert hall, though it's also used for performances of opera, dance, musical theatre and even literary readings. The 'horizons' are those of the wider world across Cardiff Bay and the Bristol Channel beyond, as well as the imaginative world of Welsh culture, whose home is here. An earlier scheme for a Cardiff Bay opera house having been attacked for its elitism, this more democratic-sounding venue was built instead.

National Museum Cardiff
CARDIFF

Right. The National Museum of Wales has a number of departments across the country, but the Cardiff-based museum in Cathays Park was the first, having opened in 1927. Displayed here is a dazzling range of exhibits: everything from a four-tonne basking shark to a Bronze-Age sword; from ammonites and earthworms to antique clothes. Since 2011, it has also been home to one of the UK's most important art collections, including Italian Renaissance and French Impressionist works alongside modern paintings and sculptures. It also boasts a broad selection of Welsh art, from the sixteenth century on.

Bute Park
CARDIFF

Next page. John Crichton-Stuart, 5th Marquess of Bute, had lived in Cardiff Castle, and in 1947 gave the grounds to a grateful city, which helps to explain the fact that a Welsh park should be named after a Scottish island. Actually, the Crichton-Stuarts had been associated with Wales and with Cardiff for some time. The 2nd Marquess had made his home in Cardiff, investing in South Wales' coal, steel and shipping industries. Though he'd risked a great deal, the profits had been enormous. His descendants, keen to give something back to the place, did so spectacularly with this park.

National Assembly for Wales
CARDIFF

Right. The Senedd, or National Assembly building, stands on the dockside, overlooking Cardiff Bay. Behind it is a visitor centre and museum. Between them, these two buildings span a century of Cardiff history, a hundred years of challenge and enterprise. When the Gothic Pierhead Building was built in 1897 as head office of the Bute Dock Company, Wales was booming and Cardiff one of the world's great ports. By the time the National Assembly was commissioned at the start of the new millennium, this was an area in need not just of democratic representation but of economic renewal.

Norwegian Church
CARDIFF

Next page. With the waters of Cardiff Bay just about passing for a fjord, this little patch of parkland off Harbour Drive has become a corner of Scandinavia. The seafarers for whom this Lutheran Church was built in the nineteenth century are long gone. Their place of worship was derelict by the 1980s and came close to being demolished, once and for all. Instead, it made a voyage of its own: taken down to make way for the Wales Millennium Centre (*see* page 216), it was reassembled on its present site, where it now serves as an arts centre.

Cardiff Castle
CARDIFF

Right. Built atop a motte (a mound of earth), a timber paling (or curtain) enclosed a central keep inside a bailey (a compound), within which soldiers could live comparatively safely in hostile territory. Thus the motte-and-bailey castle was reproduced wherever the Normans went, including here in Cardiff. The eleventh-century motte may still be seen, though the stone keep was not constructed till the 1200s. Much later, the castle (much modernized inside) became a home to the Marquesses of Bute, wealthy industrialists and shipowners.

Millennium Stadium
CARDIFF

Next page. Built for the Rugby World Cup of 1999, this magnificent stadium has since played host to an impressive variety of major events, from FA Cup Finals and Speedway Grand Prix to rock concerts. First and foremost, though, it has provided a national home to Rugby Union, a game for which Wales has historically had a passion and in which this tiny country has punched well above its weight. Whilst the opening of the stadium came after what had been a disappointing spell for the national team, it seems to have sparked a revival in the years since.

Kennixton Farmhouse, St Fagan's National History Museum

CARDIFF

Right. This seventeenth-century cottage was picked up and carried the 70 kilometres (43 miles) or so from Llangennith in the Gower to be transplanted here on the outskirts of Cardiff, with some forty other buildings. St Fagan's Castle, despite its name no more than a manor house dating from Elizabethan times, was already here, and this unique open-air museum of Welsh history was established in its grounds. Complete with nonconformist chapel, cornmill, tailor's shop, village school, saddler's workshop, smithy and even an antique urinal, it offers a wonderfully vivid experience of life in Wales down the centuries.

Castell Coch

TONGWYNLAIS, CARDIFF

Next page. There was bound to be trouble when John Crichton-Stuart, 3rd Marquess of Bute, met Thomas Burges. Both were unabashedly eccentric men of extravagantly eclectic tastes, and Burges was an architect whose designs had often as not been shunned by commissioning committees in favour of 'safer' styles. In Bute, however, he found a kindred-spirit – and an extremely wealthy one. Having maintained some semblance of sobriety in their work together on Cardiff Castle, they really let rip when it came to this Gothic Revival home outside the city.

Sugar Loaf
ABERGAVENNY, MONMOUTHSHIRE

Right. Like its namesake in Carmarthenshire (*see* page 160), the Sugar Loaf gets its name from its conical shape, though this is more apparent when it is viewed from the eastern side. Whilst the Black Mountains abut the border with England and the green fields and wooded valleys of Herefordshire, they can be strikingly wild – and feel unsettlingly remote – as we see here. Up here, wild bilberries grow; further down the mountain a vineyard produces much-praised wines. This is indeed a country of surprises.

Abergavenny Food Festival
MONMOUTHSHIRE

Next page. What Hay is to the world of books, Abergavenny is to food, and particularly the finest artisan food which is organically farmed and hand-produced. The Festival has been held every September since 1999. The local farmers who inaugurated it were making a stand in support of the British beef industry, then deeply embattled amidst the BSE crisis. Since then, the Festival has been a vital rallying point for producers in the face of everything from money-grubbing supermarkets to the mass-market ready-meal.

Clock Tower in Twyn Square
USK, MONMOUTHSHIRE

Right. The little town of Usk stands straddling the river of the same name. The crossing here has been important since the Roman era, and the bridge has been replaced a fair few times. The first to be built in stone wasn't constructed until the middle of the eighteenth century, and the present bridge was built in the 1920s. Resplendent here with displays of colourful flowers, the little clock tower in Twyn Square makes an appropriate centrepiece for a town that in the last few years has won several Britain in Bloom Awards.

Severn Bridge
CHEPSTOW, MONMOUTHSHIRE

Next page. Before this suspension bridge was opened by Queen Elizabeth II in 1966, road traffic wanting to cross had to take a ferry, or take the long way round via Gloucester, many miles upriver, adding an hour or more to the typical journey. Its central span of 988 metres (3,240 feet) slung between two towers 136 metres (445 feet) high, the bridge seemed emblematic of a Britain that was (in PM Harold Wilson's words) 'forged in the white heat of … technology'. This icon, however, has been relegated to second place: a new Severn Bridge was opened in 1996.

Tintern Abbey
TINTERN, MONMOUTHSHIRE

Right. 'And I have felt/A presence that disturbs me with the joy/Of elevated thoughts; a sense sublime….' It's interesting to note that William Wordsworth's famous poem 'Tintern Abbey' is fully entitled 'Lines composed a few miles above Tintern Abbey'; in other words, it's about a different place! Even so, generations of visitors have come to these atmospheric riverside ruins ready to hear 'the still, sad music of humanity'. And it's conceivable that they've heard it, so lovely and picturesque is the setting, so haunting the remains of this monastery sacked by Henry VIII's men in 1536.

Chepstow Castle
CHEPSTOW, MONMOUTHSHIRE

Next page. The dust from Hastings had hardly settled when work began building this great stone fortress, dramatically sited on a jagged outcrop above the River Wye. It was 1067 and William the Conqueror's lords were bustling about the kingdom consolidating Norman rule. William FitzOsbern, 1st Earl of Hereford, had been entrusted with the pacification of what was still at this point hostile territory. Hence the impressive scale of his castle here, and its immediate construction in stone (he didn't, as was customary, start out by building a fort in timber).

Roman Amphitheatre
CAERLEON, NEWPORT

Right. The Welsh name Caerleon is believed to mean 'fort of the legion'; that would certainly appear to cover the facts. Isca Augusta, as the Romans called it, was the headquarters of the Second Legion of Augustus in South Wales. What began as a camp solidified into something like a city. Wherever they were in the Roman world, legionary camps were set out in a strictly standardized pattern. When they became more permanent settlements, they tended to follow the same template. Archaeologists excavating here have found not only military fortifications, offices, barrack-blocks and granaries, but an amphitheatre (as pictured) and bathhouses as well.

Tredegar Park
NEWPORT

Next page. Tredegar House was built in the 1660s under the restored monarchy of Charles II, and embodies the values of this period to perfection. Though not, perhaps, as frivolous and foppish as some would have it, the Restoration was certainly not short of *joie de vivre*. Tredegar gives that flamboyance full expression, its construction in red brick the only mundane thing about it (though even this style was very daring in its day). The grounds are appropriately lavish, covering over 35 hectares (90 acres) in area and centred on an extensive lake. They have now become a popular public park.

Transporter Bridge
NEWPORT

Right. There's only one bridge like it in Britain, in Middlesbrough, and only a very few elsewhere in the world. Inevitably, this strange structure has become a symbol for Wales' third city. Tall, gaunt and angular in its construction, it has no roadway, but carries cars, trucks, buses and pedestrians the 235 metres (770 feet) across the River Usk in what is romantically described as a 'gondola'. Once a major shipping point for coal, a growing tourism industry is giving the lie to the assumption that Newport's industrial heritage should be dismissed as 'blight': this bridge is just one more of Wales' many wonders.

Acknowledgements

Biographies

Michael Kerrigan (author) Like so many generations of Liverpool children, Michael Kerrigan first fell in love with Wales during school trips to Colomendy, the city's camp in the Clwydian Hills. Now living in Edinburgh, he is the author of a number of travel books, including *Best-Kept Secrets of Scotland* and *Best-Kept Secrets of Paris* (both from Flame Tree). He also reviews books for the *Guardian* and the *Times Literary Supplement*.

Picture Credits

Courtesy of Shutterstock.com and the following: AP Photography 21; Bahadir Yeniceri 25, 29, 85; FatManPhoto 26; Snowshill 30; Philip Birtwistle 33; kenny1 OR ShaunWilkinson 34; Samot 37, 46, 69; Gail Johnson 38, 41, 53, 54, 58, 61, 62, 65, 82, 222, 226; stocker1970 42, 45; Darren Hedges 50; Mark Castro 57; Tony Brindley 66, 90; Erni 70; Richard Bowden 73, 210; Stephen Meese 94; AJE44 97; Steven Paul Pepper 98; rosesmith 101, 122; Kevin Eaves 109, 150, 154; Gordon Bell 110; Ms Deborah Waters 113; DaBe86 114; esinel 117; Paul Nash 118; StuartH 121, 142; Stephen Rees 125; antb 129; AdamEdwards 130; David Hughes 134; Andrew Barker 141; Anneka 145; Lian Deng 149; spectrumblue 157; Patrick Wang 158; Steve Pleydell 161, 177; Leighton Collins 165, 178; i4lcocl2 169; BasPhoto 173; Thierry Maffeis 174; Paul Cowan 181; ian woolcock 182; Remus Moise 189; JMO 198; tazzymoto 206, 217, 221, 233; Cornfield 218; Matthew Dixon 225, 230, 234; Martin Fowler 241; Joe Gough 242; Mary Lane 245.

Courtesy of SuperStock and the following: David Lyons / age fotostock 22; 81; Travel Library Limited / Travel Library Limited 93; Graham Lawrence / age fotostock 126; age fotostock 250.

© iStock.com and the following: tracy-williams-photography 49; jeffdalt 86; RobThomasson 146; vandervelden 162; jeangill 166; tirc83 170; Enfys 190; susandaniels 193; jvoisey 194, 213; aligibbs 197; liam4503 205; DigitalAllsorts 214; oversnap 229; Mike_Boyland 237; MariusBJ 246.

Courtesy of Getty Images and the following: Photographer's Choice/Jeremy Walker 74; Gallo Images/Travel Ink 89; AWL Images/John Warburton-Lee 102; VisitBritain/Britain on View 133; Universal Images Group/Geography Photos 153; Britain On View/Graham Bell 201; Stockbyte/Graham Bell 202; Britain On View/Graham Bell 209; Photolibrary/Huw Jones 238; Universal Images Group/MyLoupe 249; age fotostock/Chris Warren 253.

Index